Send
Judah First

Let your Praises Go up First
to See the Mighty Move of GOD

Gerard Assey

Send Judah First:
Let your Praises Go up First to See the Mighty Move of GOD

By
Gerard Assey

Published by:
Gerard Assey
19/18, Palli Arasan Street
Anna Nagar East
Chennai - 600 102

ISBN: 978-81-983515-3-1

Table of Contents

Preface

From the beginning of time, worship has been the heartbeat of heaven. It is the sound that filled the courts of God before the world was formed, and it is the sound that will continue for all eternity as the redeemed stand before the throne, crying, “Holy, holy, holy is the Lord God Almighty” (Revelation 4:8). Worship is not just a ritual or a religious act—it is the very essence of our relationship with God. It is the language of heaven, the battle cry of victory, and the pathway to divine encounters.

The inspiration for this book came from a powerful biblical principle: **Send Judah First.** In Scripture, Judah was not just the name of a tribe but a prophetic declaration. **"Judah" means praise**, and throughout the Bible, we see that whenever God’s people faced battles, needed direction, or sought His presence, they were instructed to **send Judah first.** Praise was not an afterthought—it was the key to unlocking divine intervention.

One of the most striking examples is found in 2 Chronicles 20, where King Jehoshaphat faced a vast enemy army. Instead of sending warriors armed with swords and shields, he sent singers and worshippers ahead of the battle line, declaring, "Give thanks to the Lord, for His mercy endures forever." As they lifted their voices, the Lord set ambushes against their enemies, and victory was won without them even lifting a weapon. This is the power of praise—it goes ahead of us, paving the way for God to move in supernatural ways.

Throughout the pages of this book, we will explore how praise is not just an act of devotion but a spiritual strategy. We will journey through the Scriptures, uncovering how worship led to breakthroughs for God's people—from the walls of Jericho crumbling at the sound of a shout to Paul and Silas being set free from prison as they sang in the midnight hour. We will also look at how Jesus Himself lived a life of worship, using praise as a foundation for miracles and breakthroughs.

But this book is not just about history; it is about practical application in our daily lives. In today's world, we face battles of our own—spiritual, emotional, and physical struggles that often seem overwhelming. Yet, the principle remains the same: when we send Judah first, we shift the atmosphere, we invite heaven's power, and we walk into divine victory.

If you have ever felt stuck, defeated, or desperate for a move of God, this book is for you. If you are a worshipper, a leader, or someone hungry for a deeper understanding of how praise can unlock supernatural encounters, this book will equip you with biblical truths and practical applications to make worship a lifestyle rather than just a Sunday activity.

As you read these pages, my prayer is that the Spirit of God will ignite a new fire in your heart—a hunger to praise Him no matter the circumstance, a desire to let worship lead your life, and a deep conviction that when you send Judah first, you will encounter the powerful move of God like never before.

Let's embark on this journey together.

Let praise rise, let heaven respond, and let victory manifest as we send Judah first!

In His Presence,

The Power of Praise before the Battle

The Command: "Judah Shall Go Up First" (Judges 1:2)

The book of Judges opens at a critical moment in Israel's history. Joshua, the mighty leader who had led the people into the Promised Land, was gone. Now, the tribes of Israel faced the daunting task of driving out the remaining Canaanites who still occupied the land. It was a time of transition, uncertainty, and battle. The Israelites sought the Lord's guidance, asking, "Who shall go up first for us against the Canaanites, to fight against them?"

The Lord's answer was clear and deliberate:

"Judah shall go up first." (Judges 1:2)

This was not just a military strategy; it was a spiritual revelation that still applies today. Judah was not the firstborn of Jacob, nor was it the largest or most powerful tribe. Yet, God instructed Judah to lead the charge. Why? Because Judah's name carried a divine key—**Judah means "praise."**

God was revealing an unshakable principle: ***before the battle, before the breakthrough, before the victory—praise must go up first.***

Understanding Judah's Name and Its Prophetic Significance

The name *Judah* comes from the Hebrew word **"Yadah"**, which means ***"to praise, to give thanks, to confess the greatness of God."*** It was a name born out of Leah's deep longing and personal transformation. When she bore Judah, she declared: "This time, I will praise the Lord." (Genesis 29:35)

Leah had spent years trying to win the affection of her husband, Jacob, as Jacob deeply loved her sister Rachel more than her. With each child she bore, she had hoped Jacob would love her. But by the time she had Judah, something changed. She was no longer focused on Jacob's approval—her focus had shifted to God.

This is the essence of true praise. It is not dependent on circumstances. It is not about seeking the validation of others. Praise is a declaration of trust, a proclamation of faith, and a surrender to God's sovereignty. Judah's name was prophetic—he was destined to lead, not just in battle, but in worship.

This is why, centuries later, when Israel inquired of the Lord about battle, God's answer was **"Judah shall go up first."** God was establishing a pattern: ***Praise must always precede the fight.***

The Spiritual Strategy of Praise Before Battle

Praise is not just a preliminary act before the real fight begins—it is a weapon of war in itself. In the natural, it may seem illogical to send singers and worshippers ahead of trained soldiers. But in the kingdom of God, spiritual battles are not won by human strength—they are won through faith, obedience, and the power of worship.

One of the most powerful examples of this is found in 2 Chronicles 20. King Jehoshaphat and the people of Judah were surrounded by a vast army. Outnumbered and seemingly doomed, Jehoshaphat sought the Lord in prayer and fasting. God's response was clear:

"Do not be afraid or discouraged because of this vast army. For the battle is not yours, but God's" (2 Chronicles 20:15)

Then, in an act of radical obedience, Jehoshaphat appointed singers to go ahead of the army, praising the Lord with these words:

"Give thanks to the Lord, for His love endures forever." (2 Chronicles 20:21)

As they sang and praised, the Lord set ambushes against their enemies, and they turned on each other. By the time Judah arrived at the battlefield, their enemies had already been defeated.

This was no accident. Praise shifts the battle from the natural to the supernatural. It invites the presence of God into the fight.

We see this again in the New Testament. Paul and Silas, beaten and imprisoned in a dungeon, chose to praise instead of despair. As they worshipped, God sent an earthquake that shook the foundations of the prison, flung the doors open, and set them free (Acts 16:25-26).

Praise doesn't just bring personal breakthrough—it affects the atmosphere around us. It opens prison doors, breaks chains, and ushers in divine intervention.

Why This Book? Who Is It For?

This book is for those who are in a battle. It is for those who have been fighting in their own strength and are ready to shift their strategy to one of worship. It is for those who long to understand the **spiritual power of praise** and how it can transform their circumstances, their mindset, and their destiny.

In the following chapters, we will explore:

- ✓ *The power of Judah's lineage—how the tribe of praise became the tribe of kings, ultimately leading to Jesus, the Lion of the tribe of Judah.*

- ✓ *The deeper meanings behind Judah's sons and how each one represents a dimension of praise.*
- ✓ *How praise is not just a response to victory, but the key to victory.*
- ✓ *How worship shifts atmospheres, dismantles demonic strongholds, and brings divine strategy.*

This is not just a book about singing songs. It is a book about spiritual warfare, kingdom principles, and the power of lifting high the name of God. It is about learning to send Judah first in every situation—before making decisions, before facing opposition, before stepping into the unknown.

If you have ever found yourself in a season of battle, uncertainty, or waiting, this book will equip you with a biblical strategy to praise your way to victory.

Final Thoughts: Send Judah First!

God's command in Judges 1:2 is still His command today. Whatever battle you are facing, whatever obstacles stand in your way—praise must go first. Not as an afterthought. Not as a mere formality. But as a deliberate, faith-filled act of surrender and warfare.

The enemy fears a praising believer. Satan wants to silence your song because he knows that where there is praise, there is power.

Will you choose to send Judah first? Will you let your praises rise before you see the breakthrough? If so, you are about to discover that when Judah goes up first, victory is inevitable.

Reflection Questions

- ✓ *How do you currently approach battles in your life—through worry, human effort, or through praise?*
- ✓ *Can you think of a time when praise changed your situation? How did God move?*
- ✓ *What would it look like for you to "send Judah first" in a specific challenge you are facing right now?*
- ✓ *Why do you think praise is such a powerful weapon in spiritual warfare?*
- ✓ *How can you cultivate a lifestyle of praise, even before you see your breakthrough?*

Who is Judah? The Tribe of Praise

The Birth of Judah – A Name Born in Praise

The story of Judah begins long before he became a mighty tribe in Israel. It begins in the heart of a woman who had known only rejection and sorrow. Leah, the first wife of Jacob, was unloved. She had been given to Jacob through deception, tricked into a marriage he never desired. While her younger sister, Rachel, captured Jacob's heart, Leah lived in the shadow of that love, longing for his affection.

God saw Leah's pain. He blessed her with children, hoping that through them, she would find the love she so deeply craved. With the birth of her first son, she named him Reuben ("See, a son!")—perhaps Jacob will now see her. When her second son, Simeon, arrived, she thought, "God has heard that I am unloved." With her third, Levi, she declared, "Now my husband will be attached to me."

But nothing changed.

It wasn't until her fourth son that something within Leah shifted. This time, there was no mention of Jacob. No desire for his approval. No longing for his love. Instead, she simply said, *"This time, I will praise the Lord."* And she named him **Judah**, meaning **"praise."** (Genesis 29:35).

Judah's birth was not just another addition to Leah's family—it was a declaration. It was a revelation that praise is not based on circumstances or human approval but is rooted in recognizing the goodness of God. This son, born out of Leah's surrender, would become the one through whom kings would arise, through whom Jesus Christ, the Lion of Judah, would come. From the very beginning, Judah's destiny was tied to praise—a destiny that would shape the future of Israel.

Judah: The Leading Tribe of Israel

Judah was the fourth son, not the firstborn. By tradition, the firstborn should have held the highest honor and inheritance, yet Judah's older brothers—Reuben, Simeon, and Levi—disqualified themselves due to sin and poor choices. God chose Judah to take the lead.

As Israel grew into a nation, Judah's position became one of prominence. In Numbers 10:14, when the Israelites set out in formation in the wilderness, Judah always marched first. They were not the largest tribe, nor the most skilled in battle at that time, but they led because their name carried a deeper truth: praise goes before victory.

Later, when Israel entered the Promised Land and sought the Lord's direction in battle, the Lord declared, **"Judah shall go up first"** (Judges 1:2). Again, God was showing that victory is not won through strength alone—it is secured **through** praise, faith, and obedience.

The Prophetic Blessing of Jacob on Judah

Before Jacob died, he gathered his sons and spoke prophetic words over each of them. When he came to Judah, his words carried a divine weight:

"Judah, you are he whom your brothers shall praise;
Your hand shall be on the neck of your enemies;
Your father's children shall bow down before you.
Judah is a lion's whelp;
From the prey, my son, you have gone up.
He bows down, he lies down as a lion;
And as a lion, who shall rouse him?

The scepter shall not depart from Judah,
Nor a lawgiver from between his feet,
Until Shiloh comes;
And to Him shall be the obedience of the people."
(Genesis 49:8-10)

This was no ordinary blessing. This was a **declaration of royalty, victory, and divine authority**.

"Your brothers shall praise you." Judah's destiny was to be exalted among the tribes.

"Your hand shall be on the neck of your enemies." Judah would be a warrior tribe, victorious over its foes.

"The scepter shall not depart from Judah." Here lies the greatest prophecy of all—**from Judah would come the kings of Israel, culminating in Jesus Christ, the King of Kings.**

Jacob's words were fulfilled when King David, the man after God's own heart, arose from the tribe of Judah. But the prophecy reached its ultimate fulfillment in **Jesus, the Messiah, the Lion of Judah.** (Revelation 5:5).

Judah and Kingship – The Line of the Messiah

Judah's lineage carried the kings of Israel. David, Solomon, and the entire line of righteous (and sometimes unrighteous) kings all came from Judah. This was not just about earthly rule; it was about something much greater. The kingdom of Judah was a foreshadowing of the eternal kingdom of Jesus Christ.

When the Apostle John had a vision of heaven in Revelation, he saw a scroll in God's hand, sealed with seven seals. A mighty angel cried out, *"Who is worthy to open the scroll and to loose its seals?"* No one in heaven or earth was found worthy, and John wept. But then, one of the elders said:

"Do not weep. Behold, the Lion of the tribe of Judah, the Root of David, has prevailed to open the scroll and to loose its seven seals." (Revelation 5:5)

Jesus is the fulfillment of Jacob's blessing on Judah. He is the eternal King, the one who holds the scepter, the lion who reigns with power and authority. The name Judah (praise) finds its ultimate purpose in Christ, because true praise always leads us to Jesus.

Judah's Role in the Wilderness – Leading the Way

In Numbers 10:14, we see another powerful demonstration of Judah's role. As the Israelites traveled through the wilderness, Judah always went first. The tabernacle of meeting, the very presence of God, was carried by the Levites in the center of the formation, but Judah was positioned in front. This was not a coincidence. The presence of God follows praise.

Even today, when we lift up praise, we are leading the way for God's presence to move. Praise makes a way for miracles. Praise clears the path for divine intervention. It is no wonder that when the Israelites sought direction in battle, God commanded, "Send Judah first."

Final Thoughts – The Power of Praise in Our Lives

Judah's story is not just history—it is a spiritual blueprint for us today.

Praise shifts our focus from ourselves to God. Like Leah, when we stop striving for human approval and start praising, we step into divine destiny.

Praise leads the way to victory. Like Judah in battle, when we lift our voices in worship, we invite God to fight for us.

Praise is the pathway to Jesus. The Lion of Judah, Jesus Christ, reigns in the praises of His people.

What battles are you facing today? Instead of fear, try praising. Instead of striving, start worshipping. Send Judah first, and watch God move.

Reflection Questions

- ✓ *What does Leah's transformation in naming Judah teach us about the power of praise in difficult seasons?*
- ✓ *How does Judah's role in leading the tribes reflect how we should approach spiritual battles today?*
- ✓ *In what areas of your life do you need to "send Judah first" before trying to fight on your own?*
- ✓ *How does knowing that Jesus is the Lion of Judah deepen your understanding of His authority and power?*
- ✓ *How can you cultivate a lifestyle of praise, even before seeing victory?*

The Sons of Judah and the Prophetic Meaning of Their Names

A fascinating key verse that highlights the effects of praise is 1 Chronicles 4:1, listing the five sons of Judah:

1. *Perez*
2. *Hezron*
3. *Carmi*
4. *Hur*
5. *Shobal*

If Judah means praise, then what do the sons of Judah symbolize? These five names reveal the five essential effects of praise in our lives.

1) Perez: Breakthrough and Victory

The Hebrew meaning of Perez is "*to break forth.*" Praise leads to breakthroughs and victories! Many people enter God's presence with distress, but as they praise, they find their release.

Biblical Examples of Breakthrough Praise:

- ✓ **Sarah:** When she surrendered to God, Isaac was born (Genesis 21:1-3).
- ✓ **David:** His praise led to victories over lions, giants, and enemies (1 Samuel 17:45-50).
- ✓ **Moses:** His obedience and worship brought about the miraculous parting of the Red Sea (Exodus 14:21-22).

2 Chronicles 20: The Power of Praise in Battle

Jehoshaphat faced a vast army, yet God told him: "The battle is not yours, but the Lord's" (2 Chronicles 20:15). Instead of sending warriors, Jehoshaphat placed singers at the front line, praising God. As they sang, God set ambushes, and their enemies destroyed themselves.

2 Chronicles 20:22 says: *"When they began to sing and praise, the Lord set ambushes..."* When we break through in praise, God breaks forth to give us victory (Perez).

2) Hezron: Protection and Security

The Hebrew meaning of Hezron is *"courtyard"* or *"a walled place of protection."* Praise creates a divine shield around us.

- ✓ **Job:** A worshipper who had divine protection (Job 1:10).
- ✓ **The Three Hebrew Boys (Daniel 3):** Shadrach, Meshach, and Abednego were thrown into the fiery furnace, but their praise brought God into the fire with them! The flames could not touch them.
- ✓ **Paul and Silas (Acts 16:25-26):** Imprisoned but still praising, they experienced divine protection and miraculous deliverance.

When we praise, God places a hedge of protection around us (Hezron).

3) Carmi: Growth and Fruitfulness

Carmi in Hebrew means *"vineyard keeper."* Praise leads to spiritual growth, abundance, and productivity in our lives.

If we do not praise God, the devil will steal our worship. Revelation 13:4 warns that the enemy seeks praise for himself.

Romans 1:21 teaches that failing to worship God leads to darkness and sin.

Jeremiah 30:19: *"Out of them shall proceed thanksgiving… and I will glorify them, and they shall not be small."*

When we praise, our lives become fruitful and blessed (Carmi).

4) Hur: Purity and Holiness
Hur means *"white linen,"* symbolizing holiness. True praise brings about purity in our lives.
Psalm 22:3: *"God inhabits the praises of His people."* His presence refines us.
1 Peter 5:6: Humility and praise keep us from pride.
David's Wife Michal (2 Samuel 6:16-23): She mocked David's worship and was struck with barrenness.
If we struggle with sin, the issue is not just morality but a lack of praise! Worship keeps us humble and focused on God's holiness.
When we praise, God purifies and sanctifies us (Hur).

5) Shobal: Overflowing Blessings
Shobal means *"overflowing like a wedding gown's train."* Praise brings supernatural overflow into our lives.
Joshua 6: The Israelites' praise brought down Jericho's walls, leading to overwhelming victory.
Isaiah 12:1-3: Praise unlocks the anointing and abundance of the Holy Spirit.
Praise Moves the Hand of God
Praise has been called *"the slender nerve that moves the mighty hand of God."*
When we praise, we step into overflowing blessings (Shobal).

Conclusion: The Power of Praise

Praise is not just an emotional expression—it is a supernatural force that transforms our lives! The five sons of Judah reveal five incredible effects of praise:

Perez – Praise brings breakthrough and victory.
Hezron – Praise builds divine protection.
Carmi – Praise fosters growth and fruitfulness.
Hur – Praise purifies and sanctifies us.
Shobal – Praise leads to overflowing blessings.

Let us be a people of praise, for when we break through in praise, God breaks forth in power!

Reflection Questions

- ✓ *How often do I intentionally praise God in my daily life? What changes when I do?*
- ✓ *In what areas of my life do I need a breakthrough? How can I apply the principle of "Perez" (Breakthrough Praise) in those situations?*
- ✓ *Have I experienced God's protection through praise (Hezron)? If not, how can I start trusting God's shield through worship?*
- ✓ *What kind of spiritual fruit (Carmi) do I see in my life? How can I cultivate a lifestyle of praise to increase fruitfulness?*
- ✓ *Do I view praise as a way to grow in holiness (Hur)? How does my worship align with a heart of purity?*
- ✓ *Have I seen the overflow of blessings (Shobal) as a result of praising God? If not, what might be hindering me from experiencing it?*
- ✓ *Which of the five effects of praise—Breakthrough, Protection, Fruitfulness, Purity, or Overflow—do I need to focus on the most right now? How can I take action?*

Praise Goes First
The Strategy of GOD

Throughout the Bible, a divine strategy emerges—one that defies human logic and turns the expected order of battle upside down. God repeatedly commands that praise should go first, setting a pattern that reveals the supernatural power of worship. Unlike earthly military tactics, where the strongest warriors and skilled fighters lead the charge, the kingdom of God operates on a higher principle: when praise goes first, victory follows.

The Biblical Pattern: Judah Goes First

The significance of praise preceding battle is first established in Judges 1:2. After the death of Joshua, the Israelites sought the Lord's direction on who should lead them into battle against the Canaanites. The Lord answered decisively: *"Judah shall go up first. Behold, I have given the land into his hand."* (Judges 1:2, ESV). This instruction was not arbitrary—it carried profound spiritual meaning. Judah, whose name means *"praise,"* was designated to lead because victory was tied to worship.

This pattern was not limited to one battle or one moment in history. It was a divine principle meant to be repeated, showing that when God's people prioritize praise, they open the door for His intervention.

Example 1: Judges 1:2 – Judah Leads Israel Into Battle

In Judges 1, Israel was at a critical juncture, stepping into new battles and territories after Joshua's leadership. Their natural instinct may have been to rely on military strategy or the might of their warriors, but God's answer pointed them to something greater: Judah. By sending Judah first, the Israelites were not just following military instructions but engaging in an act of faith—declaring that their strength came from the Lord and not from their weapons.

The result? Judah's obedience led to decisive victories. God fought on their behalf, and their enemies were delivered into their hands. This historical account reminds us that when we put praise first, we acknowledge God as the source of our strength and invite Him into our battles.

Example 2: 2 Chronicles 20 – Jehoshaphat Sends the Worshippers Ahead

One of the most dramatic examples of praise as a spiritual strategy is found in 2 Chronicles 20. King Jehoshaphat of Judah faced an overwhelming enemy—an alliance of Moabites, Ammonites, and Meunites marching against his people. Outnumbered and facing certain destruction, Jehoshaphat sought the Lord in prayer.

God's answer was unexpected but powerful: *"Do not be afraid or dismayed at this great horde, for the battle is not yours but God's"* (2 Chronicles 20:15). Instead of deploying the strongest warriors first, Jehoshaphat obeyed the divine strategy—he sent singers and worshippers ahead of the army, declaring, *"Give thanks to the Lord, for His steadfast love endures forever"* (2 Chronicles 20:21).

As the praises of Judah rang out, something miraculous happened. The enemy armies turned against one another, utterly destroying themselves. By the time Judah's army arrived, they found only the remains of a battle already won by the hand of God. This account is one of the greatest biblical demonstrations of how praise confuses the enemy and secures divine victory.

The Spiritual Warfare of Praise – Confusing the Enemy

Why is praise such a powerful weapon in spiritual warfare? Because the enemy cannot comprehend it. Satan operates in fear, doubt, and chaos—he expects people to respond to trials with worry, complaints, and despair. But when believers respond with praise instead, it disrupts his plans and shifts the atmosphere.

In Acts 16, Paul and Silas were imprisoned, beaten, and shackled in a dungeon. Instead of despairing, they chose to worship, singing hymns to God in the midnight hour. Suddenly, a divine earthquake shook the prison, opening every door and breaking every chain (Acts 16:25-26). Their praise unlocked supernatural deliverance, demonstrating that when God's people lift their voices in worship, prison doors open, and the enemy's hold is broken.

How Praise Opens the Door for Divine Intervention

The consistent pattern throughout Scripture is that praise precedes the move of God. When we praise, we are not just singing songs; we are making a faith declaration that God is sovereign over every situation. Praise shifts our focus from our problems to His power. It aligns our hearts with His purposes, making room for His presence to dwell among us.

Psalm 22:3 declares, *"Yet you are holy, enthroned on the praises of Israel."* This means that when we lift up worship, God takes His rightful place as King over our battles. His presence enters, His power is revealed, and His glory manifests in ways beyond our imagination.

Reflection Questions:

- ✓ *Can you recall a time when praising God in a difficult situation brought breakthrough or peace?*
- ✓ *How can you intentionally send praise ahead before facing challenges in your own life?*
- ✓ *What lessons can we learn from Jehoshaphat's strategy of putting worshippers in front of the battle?*
- ✓ *In what ways does praise challenge the plans of the enemy in your life?*
- ✓ *How can you cultivate a lifestyle where praise is your first response rather than a last resort?*

The divine strategy remains unchanged: Praise goes first. When we understand this principle and apply it in our lives, we position ourselves for supernatural victories. Whatever battle you may be facing today, take a step of faith—let Judah go up first!

The Lion of Judah-JESUS and the Power of Worship

From the very beginning, the tribe of Judah was set apart for leadership, power, and praise. This destiny finds its ultimate fulfillment in Jesus Christ, who is revealed in Revelation 5:5 as *"the Lion of the tribe of Judah, the Root of David, who has triumphed."* Understanding Jesus as the Lion of Judah unveils the power of worship, not just as a human response to God but as a divine strategy for victory, breakthrough, and transformation.

JESUS as the Lion of the Tribe of Judah

The image of Jesus as a lion conveys His authority, strength, and sovereignty. The lion, as the king of beasts, symbolizes dominion, courage, and unwavering power. When John wept in Revelation 5, seeing no one worthy to open the scroll, the angel reassured him: *"Do not weep! See, the Lion of the tribe of Judah, the Root of David, has triumphed"* (Revelation 5:5, NIV). This passage underscores Jesus' ultimate victory over sin, death, and the forces of darkness. Just as a lion leads with confidence and strikes fear in its enemies, Jesus reigns with unmatched power, bringing redemption to all who call upon His name.

Worship in the Life of JESUS

Although Jesus is the Lion of Judah, He also demonstrated a life of deep humility and constant worship. Unlike earthly kings who demand praise, Jesus lived a life centered on glorifying the Father. His every action—whether through prayer, thanksgiving, or song—pointed to the importance of worship.

One of the most striking moments of praise in Jesus' ministry was during His triumphal entry into Jerusalem. As He rode into the city on a donkey, fulfilling prophecy, the crowds cried out: *"Hosanna to the Son of David! Blessed is He who comes in the name of the Lord! Hosanna in the highest!"* (Matthew 21:9, ESV). The people instinctively responded with praise, welcoming their King. However, when the Pharisees urged Jesus to silence them, He replied, *"I tell you, if they keep quiet, the stones will cry out"* (Luke 19:40, NIV). This statement emphasizes that worship is not optional—it is an integral part of creation itself. If people do not praise, nature will.

JESUS used Worship to Release Miracles

One of the most profound ways Jesus demonstrated the power of worship was through His use of thanksgiving before performing miracles. In John 11:41-44, before raising Lazarus from the dead, Jesus did not immediately command life to return to Lazarus' body. Instead, He lifted His eyes to heaven and said, *"Father, I thank you that you have heard me. I knew that you always hear me, but I said this for the benefit of the people standing here, that they may believe that you sent me."* After this declaration of faith-filled worship, He called Lazarus forth, and the dead man came back to life.

Similarly, at the feeding of the five thousand (Matthew 14:19-21), Jesus took the small portion of bread and fish, looked up to heaven, and gave thanks. It was after this act of worship that multiplication occurred. This pattern reveals that worship and thanksgiving create an atmosphere for divine intervention. Jesus was demonstrating that before the miraculous is manifested, praise must go forth.

The Power of Praise in Spiritual Warfare

As the Lion of Judah, Jesus embodies the truth that worship is not just a religious exercise but a weapon of war. In the wilderness, when Satan tempted Him, Jesus responded not with debate but with the Word of God (Matthew 4:1-11). His unwavering devotion to the Father silenced the enemy. Likewise, when believers engage in worship, they proclaim Jesus' lordship and nullify the enemy's attacks. Worship shifts the atmosphere, ushering in the presence of God and dismantling darkness.

Living in the Power of the Lion of Judah

Understanding Jesus as the Lion of Judah should transform how believers approach worship. It is not a passive activity but an active engagement with the King of kings. Worship opens doors, breaks chains, and releases divine strategies. When we praise, we invite the Lion to roar over our battles, declaring His victory on our behalf.

Reflection Questions:

- ✓ *How does understanding Jesus as the Lion of Judah change your perspective on worship?*
- ✓ *In what ways can you cultivate a lifestyle of praise, following Jesus' example?*
- ✓ *Have you experienced moments when worship led to a breakthrough in your life? What happened?*
- ✓ *What are some areas in your life where you need to let praise go before the battle?*

- ✓ *How can you use thanksgiving and worship to build faith before expecting a miracle?*

Worship is more than just a song—it is a declaration of faith, a battle strategy, and a gateway to God's presence. As you embrace the power of praise, may you experience the Lion of Judah moving mightily in your life!

Praise is a Weapon-Breaking Chains in Worship

From the beginning of time, praise has been more than just an act of worship—it has been a powerful spiritual weapon. When God's people lift their voices in praise, the atmosphere shifts, the enemy is confused, and strongholds are broken. Praise is not just an expression of gratitude; it is a declaration of faith, a battle cry, and a force that brings divine intervention. The Word of God is filled with examples of how praise has shattered barriers, unlocked prison doors, and brought forth supernatural breakthroughs.

Praise Shifts the Atmosphere and Releases Breakthroughs

Praise is a mighty force that changes circumstances, not because of the sounds we make, but because of the One to whom we direct our praise. When we praise, we invite the presence of God into our situations. The Psalmist declares, *"But You are holy, enthroned in the praises of Israel"* (Psalm 22:3, NKJV). When God is enthroned in our praise, His power is made manifest, and His presence brings deliverance.

In the face of trials, praise should be our first response, not our last resort. Too often, we praise after we see the victory, but the biblical principle is to praise *before* the breakthrough. When we lift up praise in faith, we activate the supernatural power of God, shifting the battle from our hands to His. This principle is clearly illustrated in two powerful biblical examples: the deliverance of Paul and Silas from prison and the fall of Jericho's walls.

Example 1: Paul and Silas in Prison (Acts 16:25-26)

One of the most striking examples of praise breaking chains is found in the book of Acts. Paul and Silas had been unjustly arrested, beaten, and thrown into the inner dungeon of a Philippian prison. Their hands and feet were bound in stocks, their bodies aching from the wounds they had received. Most people would have sunk into despair, but instead, they chose to sing.

"About midnight Paul and Silas were praying and singing hymns to God, and the other prisoners were listening to them. Suddenly there was such a violent earthquake that the foundations of the prison were shaken. At once all the prison doors flew open, and everyone's chains came loose" (Acts 16:25-26, NIV).

Their praise triggered a supernatural earthquake. The prison doors swung open, and every prisoner's chains fell off. The jailer, witnessing this miracle, fell trembling before Paul and Silas and asked how he could be saved. That night, not only were Paul and Silas set free, but the jailer and his entire household came to Christ.

What does this teach us? Praise has the power to break chains—both physical and spiritual. It does not matter how dark the situation is or how bound we may feel; when we lift our voices in praise, the power of God is released, and freedom follows.

Example 2: Joshua and the Walls of Jericho (Joshua 6)

The story of Jericho is another powerful testament to the weapon of praise. God had promised the Israelites the land, but the fortified city of Jericho stood in their way. It seemed impossible to penetrate the mighty walls that surrounded it. Yet, God did not instruct Joshua to use weapons, ladders, or battering rams. Instead, He commanded His people to march in silence for six days and, on the seventh day, to let out a great shout of praise.

"When the trumpets sounded, the army shouted, and at the sound of the trumpet, when the men gave a loud shout, the wall collapsed; so everyone charged straight in, and they took the city" (Joshua 6:20, NIV).

What brought down the walls? Praise. The Israelites' obedience to God's instruction, coupled with their unified sound of worship, released a supernatural force that caused the walls to crumble. Their victory did not come from military strategy but from their act of faith in praising God before they saw the breakthrough.

This story teaches us that sometimes, the battles we face cannot be won by human effort alone. When we lift up a shout of praise, the walls of opposition, fear, and doubt come crashing down.

The Power of Singing, Dancing, and Shouting in Spiritual Warfare

Throughout Scripture, we see that praise is not always quiet or passive. It is often loud, expressive, and full of movement. The Bible encourages singing, dancing, and shouting as powerful expressions of worship that release spiritual breakthroughs.

- ✓ **Singing:** The Psalms are filled with calls to sing to the Lord. Singing worship songs shifts our focus from our problems to God's power.
- ✓ **Dancing:** King David danced before the Lord with all his might (2 Samuel 6:14), unashamed

of his passionate worship. His dance signified his victory and joy in God's presence.

- ✓ **Shouting:** The Hebrew word *rua* means a triumphant shout, a battle cry. Psalm 47:1 declares, *"Clap your hands, all you nations; shout to God with cries of joy!"* A shout of praise can release the power of God in ways we cannot see.

Personal Testimonies of Breakthrough Through Praise

Throughout history, believers have experienced supernatural breakthroughs through praise. Many have testified of financial miracles, healing, deliverance from addiction, and restoration of relationships after choosing to praise God in faith. Worship leaders often recount moments when the very atmosphere shifted as people engaged in heartfelt praise, bringing healing and transformation to entire congregations. Praise is not just an action; it is an invitation for God to move mightily in our lives.

Reflection Questions for Personal Application

- ✓ *What "chains" in your life need to be broken? How can you use praise as a weapon in these situations?*
- ✓ *Have you ever experienced a breakthrough after praising God? What happened?*
- ✓ *How can you cultivate a lifestyle of praise, even in difficult circumstances?*
- ✓ *What lessons can you learn from Paul and Silas, Joshua, and the walls of Jericho regarding the power of praise?*

- ✓ *Are there specific songs or scriptures that help you shift your focus to God in times of battle? How can you use them more intentionally?*

Praise is not just a response to victory; it is the key to victory. As we embrace the power of praise in every circumstance, we will see God move in ways we never imagined. Let us lift our voices, raise our hands, and declare that the battle belongs to the Lord!

Worship in Spirit and Truth
The Call to True Praise

Worship is not merely a ritual or an outward performance; it is an intimate encounter with God that stems from the depths of our hearts. Jesus emphasized this when He spoke to the Samaritan woman at the well, declaring, "But the hour is coming, and now is, when the true worshipers will worship the Father in spirit and truth; for the Father is seeking such to worship Him. God is Spirit, and those who worship Him must worship in spirit and truth" (John 4:23-24, NKJV). This profound teaching lays the foundation for understanding what true praise and worship should be.

The Difference Between Performance-Based Praise and Heartfelt Worship

There is a stark contrast between worship that is rooted in the heart and worship that is merely an act of performance. Throughout history, God's people have struggled with the temptation to offer empty sacrifices—actions that look holy but lack true devotion. Jesus rebuked the religious leaders of His day by quoting Isaiah: "These people draw near to Me with their mouth, and honor Me with their lips, but their heart is far from Me. And in vain they worship Me, teaching as doctrines the commandments of men" (Matthew 15:8-9, NKJV; Isaiah 29:13).

God does not delight in worship that is offered mechanically or for show. He desires worship that flows from a heart that truly loves and reveres Him. This kind of worship is not just about singing songs or lifting hands; it is about surrendering our entire being to Him in love and obedience.

David's Passionate Worship Before the Ark

One of the most powerful examples of genuine, heartfelt worship in the Old Testament is found in the life of King David. When the Ark of the Covenant was being brought back to Jerusalem, David could not contain his joy. Scripture tells us, "Then David danced before the Lord with all his might; and David was wearing a linen ephod" (2 Samuel 6:14, NKJV). His worship was extravagant, uninhibited, and sincere.

However, not everyone appreciated David's passionate expression of praise. His wife, Michal, despised him for his unrestrained dancing and ridiculed him for what she saw as undignified behavior. But David's response revealed the heart of a true worshiper: "It was before the Lord, who chose me… therefore I will play music before the Lord. And I will be even more undignified than this, and will be humble in my own sight" (2 Samuel 6:21-22, NKJV). David understood that worship was about exalting God, not about impressing people.

The Danger of Lip-Service Worship

Throughout the Bible, we see the dangers of worship that is empty and devoid of true devotion. The prophet Isaiah warned against this type of worship: "The Lord says: 'These people come near to me with their mouth and honor me with their lips, but their hearts are far from me. Their worship of me is based on merely human rules they have been taught'" (Isaiah 29:13, NIV).

Jesus reiterated this warning when addressing the Pharisees, highlighting that true worship is not about external rituals but about the condition of the heart. Worship that is based on tradition, routine, or mere obligation is powerless. God desires worship that is sincere, born out of love and reverence for Him.

Cultivating a Lifestyle of Worship

True worship is not confined to a Sunday service; it is a way of life. Worship should be woven into the fabric of our daily existence, influencing our thoughts, actions, and decisions. The Apostle Paul exhorts believers to present their bodies as "a living sacrifice, holy, acceptable to God, which is your reasonable service" (Romans 12:1, NKJV). This means that worship is more than a song—it is an ongoing surrender to God in every aspect of our lives.

To cultivate a lifestyle of worship, we must:

- ✓ *Develop a personal relationship with God through prayer and the Word.*
- ✓ *Worship with sincerity, whether in private or in public.*
- ✓ *Let our worship be led by the Holy Spirit, not by emotions or tradition.*
- ✓ *Honor God with our obedience and daily choices.*

Engage in acts of worship beyond music—serving others, giving generously, and living in holiness.

Reflection Questions

- ✓ *In what ways have you experienced worship as a heartfelt connection with God rather than just an outward expression?*

- ✓ *Are there areas in your life where worship has become routine rather than a genuine encounter with God?*
- ✓ *How can you cultivate a lifestyle of worship that extends beyond music and church services?*
- ✓ *What can you learn from David's example of passionate and uninhibited worship?*
- ✓ *How can you ensure that your worship is truly "in spirit and in truth" as Jesus taught?*

True worship is not about performance, ritual, or tradition—it is about intimacy with God. As we learn to worship Him in spirit and truth, we will experience the fullness of His presence and the power of true praise.

The Sound of Praise-The Role of Music in Spiritual Warfare

From the beginning of time, sound has carried power. God spoke, and the universe came into existence. The walls of Jericho fell with a shout. The heavens declare His glory, and the angels continuously cry, "Holy, holy, holy!" Praise, when lifted through music, carries a divine force that changes the atmosphere, breaks spiritual barriers, and confounds the enemy. Throughout Scripture, we see that music was never just an art form—it was a weapon, a means of deliverance, and a vessel that ushered in the presence of God.

The Power of Anointed Music to Shift Atmospheres

Music has a profound impact on the spiritual realm. When the right sound is released—one filled with true worship and the anointing of God—it can shift an environment from despair to hope, from bondage to freedom, and from fear to faith.

One of the most striking examples of this is found in 1 Samuel 16:23, where young David played the harp in King Saul's court. Saul was tormented by an evil spirit, and despite his position as king, he had no peace. But every time David played, the tormenting spirit would leave, and Saul would be refreshed.

"And it came to pass, when the evil spirit from God was upon Saul, that David took an harp, and played with his hand: so Saul was refreshed, and was well, and the evil spirit departed from him." (1 Samuel 16:23, KJV)

This verse reveals the profound effect of anointed music. It wasn't just the skill of David's playing that made the difference; it was the Spirit of God upon him. David was a man after God's own heart, and his worship carried a divine authority that drove out darkness. This teaches us that true praise, when combined with music, is not just about melody—it is a spiritual force that repels the enemy and invites the peace of God.

Why Satan Fears Worship – His Fall from Being Heaven's Chief Worshipper

To understand why music is such a powerful force in spiritual warfare, we must first examine the role of Satan before his fall. Many scholars believe that Lucifer was not just an archangel but the chief worshipper in heaven. Ezekiel 28:13-17 describes Lucifer's original state in heaven before pride led to his downfall:

"Thou hast been in Eden the garden of God; every precious stone was thy covering... the workmanship of thy tabrets and of thy pipes was prepared in thee in the day that thou wast created... Thou wast perfect in thy ways from the day that thou wast created, till iniquity was found in thee." (Ezekiel 28:13, 15 KJV)

The reference to "tabrets" (tambourines) and "pipes" suggests that Lucifer himself was created with the ability to produce worship. He was designed to glorify God, to lead the heavenly host in praise. But when he sought to elevate himself above God (Isaiah 14:12-14), he was cast down.

Because of his fall, Satan despises true worship. He knows the power that worship carries, and he seeks to divert it away from God. This is why the enemy has infiltrated music in the world, using it to influence minds, spread darkness, and lure people away from the presence of God. But when believers raise a sound of true praise, they remind Satan of everything he lost—and they establish the dominion of God in their midst.

Worship Invites the Presence of God

One of the most well-known truths in Scripture is that God inhabits the praises of His people. Psalm 22:3 **declares:**

"But thou art holy, O thou that inhabitest the praises of Israel."

When we worship, God's presence fills the place where we are. His glory descends, and where His glory is, transformation happens. This is why in times of distress, fear, or warfare, lifting a song of praise is one of the most powerful things a believer can do.

A striking example of this can be seen in 2 Chronicles 5:13-14, when Solomon dedicated the temple. The moment the singers and musicians lifted their voices in unity, the glory of God filled the temple like a cloud, so much so that the priests could not even stand to minister. The sound of praise ushered in such a weighty presence of God that everything else had to yield.

"It came even to pass, as the trumpeters and singers were as one, to make one sound to be heard in praising and thanking the Lord; and when they lifted up their voice with the trumpets and cymbals and instruments of musick, and praised the Lord... that then the house was filled with a cloud, even the house of the Lord." (2 Chronicles 5:13 KJV)

This is what happens when worshippers align themselves with heaven's sound. Whether in the temple, in a church, or in a believer's home, praise carries the authority to shift atmospheres, break strongholds, and usher in divine encounters.

The Role of Music in Personal and Corporate Worship

As believers, we must understand that music in worship is not entertainment—it is a spiritual engagement. When we sing and play instruments unto the Lord with hearts surrendered to Him, we release a sound that impacts both the natural and supernatural realms. This is why Paul exhorts the church in Ephesians 5:19 to:

"Speak to yourselves in psalms and hymns and spiritual songs, singing and making melody in your heart to the Lord."

Similarly, Colossians 3:16 encourages us to let the Word of Christ dwell richly in us, singing with grace in our hearts to the Lord. Worship in music is not an option; it is a powerful key to spiritual growth, deliverance, and intimacy with God.

Reflection Questions

- ✓ *Have you experienced a time when worship changed the atmosphere around you? What happened?*
- ✓ *In what ways do you think Satan tries to attack worship in your life? How can you guard against these distractions?*
- ✓ *How can you cultivate a deeper lifestyle of worship, where music is more than just a routine but a weapon of spiritual warfare?*
- ✓ *Are there areas in your life where you need a breakthrough? How can you use worship as a strategy to invite God's power into those situations?*

The Sacrifice of Praise- Worship in Difficult Times

There are moments in life when praising God comes naturally—when prayers are answered, doors are opened, and blessings overflow. It is easy to lift our hands and sing when we see His goodness manifested in our lives. But what about when the opposite happens? What about the moments when everything falls apart—when loss, pain, and trials come crashing in like an unrelenting storm? Can we still worship then?

The Bible speaks of *the sacrifice of praise* (Hebrews 13:15). A sacrifice is something that costs us—it is an offering given, not out of convenience, but out of conviction. True worship is not just about celebrating God when life is good; it is about choosing to praise Him even when life feels unbearable. This kind of worship is powerful because it is rooted not in circumstances but in faith.

Worshipping God in Pain, Loss, and Trials

One of the most profound examples of worship in suffering is found in the life of Job. Job was a man who feared God and lived righteously. He was blessed with wealth, health, and a loving family. But in a single day, his world collapsed. He lost his livestock, his servants, his home, and—most devastatingly—his children. One tragedy followed another, each report more crushing than the last. Yet, in that moment of overwhelming grief, Job did something astonishing.

"Then Job arose, and rent his mantle, and shaved his head, and fell down upon the ground, and

worshipped, and said, Naked came I out of my mother's womb, and naked shall I return thither: the LORD gave, and the LORD hath taken away; blessed be the name of the LORD." (Job 1:20-21, KJV)

Job's response defies human logic. Instead of cursing God, instead of questioning why, instead of allowing bitterness to take root, he worshipped. He acknowledged that everything he had was a gift from God, and even in loss, he declared that God was still worthy of praise.

This is the essence of sacrificial worship. It is worship that does not deny the pain but chooses to glorify God despite it. It is worship that says, "God, I don't understand, but I trust You." This kind of worship shakes the kingdom of darkness because it proves that our faith is not based on what God *gives* us but on *who He is.*

Habakkuk's Decision to Praise Despite No Visible Blessing

Another striking example of sacrificial praise is found in the book of Habakkuk. The prophet was witnessing devastation—his nation was falling apart, the enemy was advancing, and nothing seemed to be going right. In the natural, there was no reason to rejoice. And yet, in one of the most powerful declarations of faith in Scripture, Habakkuk chose to praise God despite what he saw.

"Although the fig tree shall not blossom, neither shall fruit be in the vines; the labour of the olive shall fail, and the fields shall yield no meat; the flock shall be cut off from the fold, and there shall be no herd in the stalls: Yet I will rejoice in the Lord, I will joy in the God of my salvation. The Lord God is my strength,

and he will make my feet like hinds' feet, and he will make me to walk upon mine high places." (Habakkuk 3:17-19, KJV)

Notice Habakkuk's words: "Yet I will rejoice." This is not praise based on emotions. It is not dependent on circumstances. This is a decision—an act of the will to worship God *even when nothing makes sense.*

Habakkuk understood something vital: worship is a declaration of faith. It is saying, "God, I may not see the answer right now, but I trust that You are still in control." True praise is not just for the mountaintop; it is a lifeline in the valley.

The Difference Between Praise Based on Feelings vs. Praise Based on Faith

There are two kinds of praise:

- ✓ Praise based on feelings – This kind of praise is emotional and dependent on circumstances. It fluctuates with the highs and lows of life. When things are good, it is easy to sing and worship. But when trials come, this kind of praise fades because it is built on the shifting sands of emotion.
- ✓ Praise based on faith – This is the kind of praise that stands firm regardless of what happens. It is deeply rooted in the unchanging character of God. It is the praise that Job gave, the praise that Habakkuk gave, the praise that Paul and Silas gave when they were locked in a prison cell, beaten and chained, yet singing at midnight (Acts 16:25).

Faith-filled praise is not about denying reality—it is about *declaring a greater reality*. It is saying, *"Yes, my situation is painful, but my God is greater. Yes, I am struggling, but my God is faithful."* This kind of worship releases breakthrough because it shifts the focus from the problem to the Problem-Solver.

The Power of Declaring God's Goodness Even in Suffering

Satan's greatest desire is to silence the praise of God's people. He knows that when believers worship—even in suffering—it weakens his grip. Why? Because praise invites the presence of God, and where God's presence is, there is freedom (Psalm 22:3, 2 Corinthians 3:17).

King David, a man who knew both victory and heartbreak, wrote these words:

"I will bless the Lord at all times: his praise shall continually be in my mouth." (Psalm 34:1, KJV)

David's commitment to continual praise was not because his life was always easy. He wrote many of his psalms while fleeing for his life, hiding in caves, and enduring deep betrayal. Yet, he refused to let circumstances dictate his worship.

Paul echoes this same truth in 1 Thessalonians 5:16-18:

"Rejoice evermore. Pray without ceasing. In everything give thanks: for this is the will of God in Christ Jesus concerning you."

Notice that Paul says, *"In everything give thanks,"* not *"For everything give thanks."* We don't thank God *for* the trials, but we thank Him *in* the trials because we know that He is still working, still faithful, and still good.

When we choose to praise in pain, something shifts. The chains that once held us in despair begin to break. The enemy's lies lose their grip. Our faith is strengthened, and we begin to see God's hand moving in ways we never expected.

This is the sacrifice of praise—worship that costs us something, but in return, brings us into the very presence of God.

Reflection Questions

- ✓ *Have you ever experienced a time when worship felt like a sacrifice? How did you respond?*
- ✓ *What lessons can you learn from Job and Habakkuk about praising God in difficult seasons?*
- ✓ *Is your praise more often based on feelings or faith? How can you cultivate a lifestyle of faith-filled worship?*
- ✓ *How can declaring God's goodness change your perspective in times of suffering?*
- ✓ *What specific steps can you take to make praise your response, even in life's hardest moments?*

Building a Lifestyle of Praise From Occasional to Continual Worship

Many people view worship as something they do once a week—reserved for Sunday mornings, a specific gathering, or moments of deep emotion. While there is certainly a place for corporate worship, true praise is far more than just a scheduled event. It is meant to be a lifestyle, a constant outpouring of our hearts toward God, not confined to a time or place but woven into the very fabric of our daily lives.

God never intended for praise to be an occasional response to His blessings; He desires that it become the very rhythm of our existence. When we shift from seeing worship as something we do to recognizing that it is *who we are*, we step into a deeper, more fulfilling relationship with Him.

Praise Is Not Just for Sundays – Cultivating a Daily Lifestyle of Worship

The way we approach praise often reveals the state of our hearts. If we only worship when things are going well, or when we are in a church setting, we limit the power of praise in our lives. A true lifestyle of worship means that regardless of where we are, what we are facing, or how we feel, we are constantly directing our hearts and minds toward God in adoration.

One of the most powerful examples of daily worship is found in the life of Daniel. Daniel was a man of excellence, wisdom, and unwavering faith. He lived in Babylon, a foreign land with foreign gods, yet he never allowed the culture around him to shape his devotion.

Even when the decree was signed forbidding prayer to anyone except the king, Daniel remained steadfast. The Bible tells us:

"Now when Daniel knew that the writing was signed, he went into his house; and his windows being open in his chamber toward Jerusalem, he kneeled upon his knees three times a day, and prayed, and gave thanks before his God, as he did aforetime." (Daniel 6:10, KJV)

Daniel's worship was not dictated by circumstances. He did not wait for a crisis to seek God, nor did he allow fear to silence his praise. His worship was a daily habit, a lifestyle. This is why, when the trial came, he did not waver—his heart was already anchored in God.

Imagine if we lived this way, if worship became as natural to us as breathing. Instead of waiting for Sunday, we would wake up in praise, go about our day in constant awareness of God's goodness, and end each night with gratitude in our hearts.

The Power of Speaking Psalms and Hymns in Daily Life

The early church understood the importance of continual praise. The apostle Paul, writing to the believers in Ephesus, gave a key to maintaining a spirit of worship:

"Speaking to yourselves in psalms and hymns and spiritual songs, singing and making melody in your heart to the Lord;" (Ephesians 5:19, KJV)

Notice that Paul encourages believers to *speak* to themselves in psalms, hymns, and spiritual songs. There is something powerful about declaring God's truth out loud. When we fill our mouths with praise, it shifts our focus from the problems of life to the greatness of God.

In the Old Testament, King David exemplified this lifestyle of praise. He was a man who faced wars, betrayal, loss, and hardship, yet his response was always to turn to God in worship. The book of Psalms is filled with his songs—many written in times of deep distress. Yet, rather than being overwhelmed by his circumstances, he chose to declare God's goodness over and over again.

One of his most well-known psalms declares:

"I will bless the Lord at all times: his praise shall continually be in my mouth." (Psalm 34:1, KJV)

David did not say, "I will bless the Lord *when things go well*." He said, *"at all times."* That means in joy and sorrow, in victory and defeat, in clarity and confusion. This is the essence of a lifestyle of praise.

When we begin to speak God's Word and sing His praises daily, it transforms us from the inside out. Praise becomes a weapon against fear, doubt, and discouragement. It realigns our hearts to the truth of who God is, keeping us spiritually strong even in the midst of trials.

The Role of Gratitude and Thanksgiving in Spiritual Maturity

Praise and gratitude are inseparable. A lifestyle of worship is impossible without a heart that is filled with thanksgiving.

Paul, writing to the church in Thessalonica, gives this command:

"In every thing give thanks: for this is the will of God in Christ Jesus concerning you." (1 Thessalonians 5:18, KJV)

Giving thanks in *everything* does not mean we ignore hardships, but it does mean we acknowledge God's goodness even in them. When we practice gratitude, our perspective shifts. Instead of focusing on what we lack, we begin to recognize God's provision in every area of our lives.

A thankful heart is a mature heart. It is a heart that understands that God is sovereign, that His plans are always good, and that He is working all things together for our good (Romans 8:28).

In the New Testament, we see this clearly in the life of Jesus. Before feeding the five thousand, what did Jesus do? He gave thanks (John 6:11). Before raising Lazarus from the dead, He thanked the Father (John 11:41). Even on the night before His crucifixion, He took bread, gave thanks, and broke it (Luke 22:19).

If Jesus, knowing what was ahead, practiced thanksgiving in all things, how much more should we? Gratitude is the foundation of continual praise. It reminds us of God's faithfulness in the past and gives us confidence for the future.

When we make gratitude a daily habit, worship becomes second nature. We stop waiting for perfect conditions to praise God and start seeing His hand in every detail of our lives.

Living a Life of Praise

Building a lifestyle of praise does not happen overnight. It is a deliberate choice we make each day—to lift our eyes to heaven instead of being consumed by the distractions of the world. It is a commitment to remember His goodness, even in trials, and to make worship our first response rather than our last resort.

When we choose to worship continually, we experience a transformation. Our faith deepens, our hearts remain tender before God, and we walk in the joy and strength that only He can provide.

Praise is not meant to be a once-a-week event; it is meant to be the heartbeat of our lives. May we be like Daniel, unwavering in our devotion, like David, praising at all times, and like Jesus, giving thanks in all circumstances.

As we do, we will discover that worship is not just something we give to God—it is something that changes *us.*

Reflection Questions

- ✓ *Is praise currently a daily habit in your life, or is it something you reserve for specific moments?*
- ✓ *What steps can you take to cultivate a lifestyle of continual worship?*
- ✓ *How does speaking psalms, hymns, and spiritual songs change your perspective and strengthen your faith?*
- ✓ *In what areas of your life do you struggle to be thankful? How can you begin to practice gratitude more consistently?*
- ✓ *Who in the Bible inspires you in their daily devotion to worship, and what lessons can you apply from their life?*

Praise and Prophetic Breakthroughs- How Worship Reveals GOD's Plans

Worship is more than just singing songs or lifting hands in reverence. It is a powerful spiritual weapon, a gateway into the supernatural, and a catalyst for divine revelation. Throughout Scripture, we see that when people worshipped, the heavens opened, God's voice was revealed, and breakthroughs took place. Worship, when done in faith, does not just remain an act of devotion—it becomes a conduit for divine strategy, guidance, and prophecy.

The connection between praise and the prophetic is undeniable. When we worship in spirit and truth, our spiritual senses are awakened, our hearts become aligned with God's will, and we begin to perceive things beyond the natural realm. Praise shifts the atmosphere, preparing a space where God's voice can be heard with clarity.

How Prophetic Worship Releases Divine Revelation

Prophetic worship is not merely about singing a setlist of songs; it is about stepping into a place where heaven invades earth. When believers engage in true, spirit-led worship, they create an environment where God's plans and purposes can be revealed. The prophetic is all about seeing into the unseen, declaring the things that are yet to come, and aligning ourselves with God's divine agenda.

The Bible gives us a powerful example of how worship sets the stage for prophetic revelation. In 2 Kings 3, the prophet Elisha found himself in the midst of a troubling situation. Three kings—Jehoram of

Israel, Jehoshaphat of Judah, and the king of Edom—were on the brink of war against Moab. However, after marching for seven days, they ran out of water and were in desperate need of divine intervention.

Jehoshaphat, a godly king, sought the counsel of a prophet, and Elisha was called. But before Elisha could deliver the word of the Lord, he asked for something significant:

"But now bring me a musician. And when the musician played, the hand of the Lord came upon him." (2 Kings 3:15, ESV)

Elisha understood something many of us overlook—worship creates a prophetic flow. He did not attempt to prophesy out of his own emotions or intellect; instead, he positioned himself in an atmosphere of worship. As the musician played, the Spirit of God came upon him, and he received divine revelation.

What happened next was extraordinary. Elisha delivered a prophetic word that defied human logic. He told the kings that, though they saw no wind or rain, God would fill the valley with water. And more than that, He would give them victory over their enemies. True to the prophecy, God supernaturally provided water, and their enemies were defeated.

This moment in Elisha's life teaches us that prophetic breakthroughs are often birthed in worship. When we enter into deep, spirit-led praise, we silence the noise of the world and tune our hearts to heaven's frequency. Worship positions us to hear clearly from God.

Why Prophetic Songs Are Essential in Churches Today

In the modern church, many people view worship as a time of singing before the sermon. While structured worship has its place, the church is in desperate need of a revival of prophetic worship—a type of worship where songs are not just sung but where heaven's agenda is declared.

Prophetic songs carry the sound of God's voice for the present moment. They break chains, shift atmospheres, and release the power of God in ways that scripted worship alone cannot. The Psalms are a perfect example of this. Many of David's psalms were not just songs of praise, but prophetic declarations of God's plans.

Consider Psalm 22, where David prophetically describes the suffering of Christ centuries before it happened:

"My God, my God, why have you forsaken me?" (Psalm 22:1, ESV)

These were the very words Jesus would cry out on the cross. David, in his worship, was unknowingly tapping into a prophetic revelation of what was to come.

The New Testament echoes this principle. Ephesians 5:19 instructs believers to be:

"Speaking to yourselves in psalms and hymns and spiritual songs, singing and making melody in your heart to the Lord." (KJV)

The early church understood that spiritual songs were more than melodies—they were prophetic utterances that built up the body of Christ. The book of Revelation also shows us glimpses of heaven, where worship is constant and carries prophetic significance. The song of the Lamb (Revelation 5:9-

10) declares Christ's victory over the nations. Worship, even in eternity, is prophetic in nature.

If the church today embraced prophetic worship, we would see a greater outpouring of the Holy Spirit, more clarity in hearing God's voice, and supernatural breakthroughs in our lives and communities.

Activating Faith Through Worship – Seeing Beyond the Natural

One of the greatest challenges in the Christian walk is learning to see beyond what our physical eyes perceive. Life often presents circumstances that seem impossible—financial struggles, sickness, broken relationships, and unanswered prayers. But faith is the ability to see beyond the natural and believe in the unseen.

The Bible says,

"Now faith is the substance of things hoped for, the evidence of things not seen." (Hebrews 11:1, KJV)

Worship plays a crucial role in activating this kind of faith. When we worship, we shift our focus from our problems to the greatness of God. We remind ourselves that He is bigger than our circumstances. Praise is an act of faith in action—declaring God's goodness before we see the breakthrough.

Consider the story of Paul and Silas in Acts 16. They were beaten, chained, and thrown into the depths of a prison. Yet, in the darkest hour of the night, they did something extraordinary:

"About midnight Paul and Silas were praying and singing hymns to God, and the prisoners were listening to them." (Acts 16:25, ESV)

What happened next was supernatural. As they worshipped, an earthquake shook the prison, the doors flung open, and their chains fell off. Their praise activated a breakthrough that could not be explained by natural means.

Faith-filled worship sees beyond the chains. It looks past the prison doors and envisions freedom. It is not limited by earthly restrictions but taps into the realm of the impossible.

Many times, our prophetic breakthrough is waiting on our praise. When we choose to lift our voices in worship, even in difficulty, we activate God's power in ways we cannot comprehend.

Living in the Prophetic Flow of Worship

To live in the prophetic flow of worship means we cultivate a lifestyle where praise is not just a routine, but a gateway into God's divine revelation. It means that when we worship, we do so with expectation—knowing that God speaks, moves, and reveals His plans through our praise.

Like Elisha, we must learn to call upon the presence of God through worship. Like David, we must allow our songs to be prophetic declarations of what God is doing and will do. Like Paul and Silas, we must praise before the breakthrough comes.

When we live this way, worship becomes more than a song—it becomes a force that shapes history, unlocks the unseen, and releases God's plans over our lives and the world.

Reflection Questions

- ✓ *How has worship helped you hear from God in the past?*
- ✓ *What steps can you take to enter into a deeper, more prophetic flow of worship?*

- ✓ *Have you ever experienced a breakthrough that came through praising God? What did you learn from it?*
- ✓ *How can the church today embrace prophetic worship more fully?*
- ✓ *What situation in your life needs a breakthrough, and how can you begin to praise God in faith before it happens?*

Judah and the End Times
The Final Song of Praise

From the very beginning of creation to the final moments of history, worship has been the defining purpose of God's people. Worship is not just something we do here on earth—it is the very essence of heaven, the eternal language of those who dwell in God's presence. Throughout the Bible, we see that worship is central to God's plan, not only in our personal lives but in the unfolding of His divine purpose for all eternity.

In the end times, when the heavens open and the King of Kings returns in glory, worship will reach its ultimate fulfillment. All of creation, from the highest angels to the humblest saints, will lift up one voice in adoration of the Lamb who was slain. This is the **final song of praise**, the everlasting anthem of victory, and the completion of what began with Judah—the tribe of praise.

The Role of Worship in Heaven

Heaven is not a place of silence. It is a realm filled with the constant sound of praise, resounding with the voices of angels, elders, and redeemed saints who declare the glory of God. The book of Revelation gives us an awe-inspiring glimpse into this heavenly worship.

John, in his vision, was transported into the throne room of God, where he witnessed worship unlike anything seen on earth. He describes:

"And the four living creatures, each of them with six wings, are full of eyes all around and within, and day and night they never cease to say, 'Holy, holy, holy,

is the Lord God Almighty, who was and is and is to come!'" (Revelation 4:8, ESV)

These four living creatures, symbolic of the highest order of angelic beings, never cease in their worship. There is no pause, no moment of silence in heaven's praise. Their worship is eternal because it is anchored in the very nature of God—His holiness, His power, and His unchanging existence.

But this heavenly worship does not stop with the angels. As the vision continues, John sees **the** twenty-four elders, representing the redeemed people of God, falling before the throne:

"They cast their crowns before the throne, saying, 'Worthy are you, our Lord and God, to receive glory and honor and power, for you created all things, and by your will they existed and were created.'" (Revelation 4:10-11, ESV)

This scene reveals an essential truth—all of heaven exists to glorify God. The elders, who hold positions of great honor, willingly lay down their crowns because even the highest position in heaven is nothing compared to the greatness of God.

This is what worship does: it removes self from the throne and places God in His rightful place.

The Song of the Redeemed – Worshiping Before the Throne

As John's vision unfolds, something incredible happens. A new song rises in heaven—not just from the angels, but from those who have been redeemed by the blood of Christ. This is the song of the Lamb, the anthem of those who have been saved:

"And they sang a new song, saying, 'Worthy are you to take the scroll and to open its seals, for you were slain, and by your blood you ransomed people for

God from every tribe and language and people and nation, and you have made them a kingdom and priests to our God, and they shall reign on the earth.'" (Revelation 5:9-10, ESV)

This song is different from anything ever sung before. It is not the song of the angels—it is the song of the redeemed. This is the song we, as believers, will one day sing in the presence of the King. It is a song of gratitude, declaring the worthiness of Jesus, who purchased our salvation with His own blood.

Imagine this moment: people from every nation, every generation, every walk of life, standing together before the throne, singing as one. No more divisions, no more pain, no more sin—just the pure, unending worship of the Lamb.

And the worship doesn't stop there. John describes how the worship intensifies until all of creation joins in:

"Then I heard every creature in heaven and on earth and under the earth and in the sea, and all that is in them, saying, 'To him who sits on the throne and to the Lamb be blessing and honor and glory and might forever and ever!'" (Revelation 5:13, ESV)

This is the final song of praise—the song that will never end. It is the fulfillment of Judah's call to praise, the destiny of all who belong to the Lord.

Why Worship Will Never Cease – It Is Our Eternal Calling

Many people think of worship as something they do on Sundays, but worship is not an event—it is an identity. The call to worship does not begin when we enter a church building, nor does it end when we leave. Worship is eternal because it is the very purpose for which we were created.

In the Old Testament, Judah was the tribe assigned to go before Israel in battle. Their name means *"praise"*, and they were the first to lead the charge. But their role was not just for earthly battles—it was a prophetic picture of what was to come. Just as Judah led Israel in victory through praise, so the redeemed of the Lord will lead eternity in worship.

When Jesus returns, the final act of history will not be war, but worship. Every knee will bow, every tongue will confess that Jesus Christ is Lord (Philippians 2:10-11). Worship is the culmination of God's plan, the great gathering of the saints, and the celebration of Christ's ultimate victory over sin and death.

Preparing Now for a Life of Praise That Echoes Into Eternity

If worship is our eternal calling, then we must ask ourselves: Are we preparing for it now?

Many believers struggle with worship, seeing it as something that depends on their emotions or circumstances. But if worship will be our eternal occupation, then we should begin cultivating a heart of praise now.

David understood this when he wrote:

"I will bless the Lord at all times; his praise shall continually be in my mouth." (Psalm 34:1, ESV)

The key word here is "continually." Praise should not be occasional—it should be constant, regardless of what we are going through.

Paul and Silas understood this when they worshipped in a prison cell (Acts 16:25). The early church understood this when they sang in times of persecution. And in the last days, those who are faithful to God will understand this as they worship even in the face of tribulation.

Worship is not just for good times. It is the key to victory, the weapon of the overcomer, and the sound of eternity breaking into the present.

If we truly believe that worship is our destiny, then we should not wait until heaven to engage in it. We must become worshippers now—not just in church, but in our daily lives. Our praise should rise in the morning, in the workplace, in the battles, and in the triumphs.

Because when the final song of praise begins, we don't want to be outsiders looking in—we want to be active participants, ready to join the eternal choir of the redeemed.

Reflection Questions

- ✓ *How does the vision of worship in heaven inspire your personal worship here on earth?*
- ✓ *In what ways can you cultivate a lifestyle of continual praise, regardless of circumstances?*
- ✓ *How does knowing that worship is eternal change your perspective on its importance today?*
- ✓ *What areas of your life need to be surrendered to God in worship?*
- ✓ *Are you preparing now to be part of the final song of praise when Jesus returns?*

The Power of Praise in Impossible Situations

Praise is a divine weapon that invites God's presence and power into impossible situations. Throughout the Bible, men and women encountered trials beyond their strength, but when they lifted their voices in praise, God moved in miraculous ways. This chapter explores ten powerful biblical examples—five from the Old Testament and five from the New Testament—where praise shifted the course of history, brought deliverance, and demonstrated God's mighty hand.

Old Testament Examples

1. Hannah's Praise Birthed a Miracle (1 Samuel 1-2)

Hannah was barren and deeply distressed. She faced ridicule from her rival, Peninnah, and sorrow filled her heart. Despite years of disappointment, she did something remarkable—she turned her anguish into worship.

At the temple, she poured out her soul before God, and after Eli the priest blessed her, she worshiped. In 1 Samuel 2:1-10, Hannah sang a song of praise, declaring God's power to raise the lowly and make the barren fruitful.

God honored her faith and praise, and in due time, she conceived and bore Samuel, one of Israel's greatest prophets. Her praise transformed an impossible situation into a testimony of God's power!

2. Miriam's Song of Deliverance at the Red Sea (Exodus 15:1-21)

The Israelites were trapped—the Red Sea before them, Pharaoh's army behind them. In the natural, there was no way out. But God miraculously parted the sea, allowing His people to cross on dry ground. When the waters returned and drowned their enemies, Moses and Miriam led Israel in a song of praise.

In Exodus 15:1-2, they sang: *"I will sing to the Lord, for He has triumphed gloriously! The horse and its rider He has thrown into the sea!"*

Their praise acknowledged God's victory and cemented His power in the hearts of the people. Worship followed deliverance, but it also reinforced faith for future battles.

3. Deborah and Barak's Victory Song (Judges 5:1-31)

Israel was under Canaanite oppression, facing an impossible war against King Jabin and his powerful commander, Sisera. But under the leadership of Deborah, the prophetess, and Barak, they went to battle, and God fought for them, routing their enemies.

After the victory, Deborah and Barak lifted a powerful song of praise in Judges 5, recounting God's mighty acts and celebrating how He had turned the tide in Israel's favor. Their song declared, *"O my soul, march on in strength!" (Judges 5:21).*

Praise was their response, but it also prepared their hearts to trust God for future triumphs.

4. Jonah's Praise Brought Him Out of the Belly of the Fish (Jonah 2:1-10)

Jonah had run from God's call and was swallowed by a great fish—a situation that seemed utterly hopeless. In the belly of darkness, Jonah did something unexpected: he praised God before the deliverance even happened.

He declared in Jonah 2:9, *"But I, with shouts of grateful praise, will sacrifice to you. What I have vowed I will make good. I will say, 'Salvation comes from the Lord.'"*

As soon as he praised, the fish released him onto dry land! His praise activated God's power to deliver him.

5. Hezekiah's Worship and Supernatural Deliverance (2 Kings 19:14-35)

The Assyrian king, Sennacherib, surrounded Jerusalem, threatening to destroy it. Hezekiah faced overwhelming odds—his army was no match for Assyria. But instead of succumbing to fear, he turned to the Lord in prayer and praise.

In response, God sent an angel who struck down 185,000 Assyrian soldiers in one night! The enemy fled without a fight.

His prayer and praise positioned him for divine intervention, proving that praise shifts the battle from human hands into God's hands.

New Testament Examples

1. Mary's Praise Released the Messiah (Luke 1:46-55)

When the angel Gabriel told Mary she would conceive Jesus, the Son of God, she responded not with fear but with praise. She lifted what is known as *The Magnificat* (Luke 1:46-55), saying:

"My soul magnifies the Lord, and my spirit rejoices in God my Savior!"

Her praise activated God's purpose in her life. It positioned her to carry the greatest miracle of all time—the birth of Christ.

2. The Leper's Gratitude and Wholeness (Luke 17:11-19)

Ten lepers were healed by Jesus, but only one returned to give Him praise. Jesus asked, *"Were not ten cleansed? But where are the nine?" (Luke 17:17).*

The one who came back received something greater—not just healing, but complete wholeness. His praise moved God's heart, bringing total restoration beyond the physical.

3. The Canaanite Woman's Worship Brought Healing (Matthew 15:21-28)

A Canaanite woman came to Jesus, desperately seeking healing for her demon-possessed daughter. Initially, Jesus remained silent, testing her faith. But instead of giving up, she knelt before Him and worshiped:

"Lord, help me!" (Matthew 15:25).

Her persistent worship moved Jesus' heart, and He granted her request, healing her daughter instantly. Her praise and worship broke through what seemed like a divine silence, bringing miraculous intervention.

4. The Blind Man's Worship Opened His Eyes (John 9:1-38)

Jesus healed a man blind from birth. The religious leaders questioned him, but he boldly praised Jesus, saying, *"One thing I know: I was blind, but now I see!" (John 9:25).*

Later, when he fully understood who Jesus was, he fell at His feet and worshiped Him (John 9:38). His praise sealed his miracle, turning physical healing into spiritual revelation.

5. The Church's Prayer and Praise Freed Peter from Prison (Acts 12:1-17)

Peter was imprisoned under heavy guard, facing execution. The church responded not with fear but with earnest prayer and praise.

As they lifted their voices, an angel appeared, chains fell off Peter, and the prison doors opened by themselves. Peter walked out unharmed, proving that praise shakes even the strongest chains.

Conclusion: Praise Unlocks the Impossible

From barren wombs to deadly prisons, from war-torn battlefields to dark fish-bellies, praise has consistently unleashed God's supernatural power. These ten stories demonstrate a divine pattern:

- ✓ *Hannah's praise turned barrenness into fruitfulness.*
- ✓ *Miriam's song confirmed miraculous deliverance.*
- ✓ *Deborah's praise celebrated God's victory.*
- ✓ *Jonah's thanksgiving triggered divine rescue.*
- ✓ *Hezekiah's worship led to angelic intervention.*
- ✓ *Mary's praise ushered in the Messiah.*
- ✓ *The leper's gratitude brought complete restoration.*
- ✓ *The Canaanite woman's worship unlocked healing.*

- ✓ *The blind man's praise confirmed his transformation.*
- ✓ *The church's prayer and praise broke prison chains.*

No matter how impossible the situation, praise shifts the atmosphere and moves the hand of God. Let us be people of praise, knowing that when we exalt His name, miracles are set in motion!

Practical Exercises for Worship Leaders: How to Lead Congregations in Judah-Style Worship

Worship is more than just a song; it is a spiritual weapon, a declaration of faith, and an invitation for God's presence to move. As a worship leader, you are not just a musician or a singer—you are a spiritual guide, leading God's people into encounters with Him. Worship has the power to break chains, shift atmospheres, and bring divine breakthrough when it is done in the spirit of Judah-style worship—a worship that is bold, declarative, and victorious.

The name Judah means "praise", and throughout the Bible, we see how Judah led the way in battle and in worship. From the Old Testament battles of Israel to the heavenly throne room in Revelation, praise always goes first. This chapter provides practical exercises to help worship leaders develop the skills, sensitivity, and spiritual authority to lead worship in a way that brings transformation.

---

1. Cultivating a Judah Mindset: Leading with Expectation

Before you can lead others in Judah-style worship, you must first develop a **Judah mindset**—a heart that expects God to move when you praise Him.

Exercise: The Praise Before the Breakthrough

Biblical Example: *2 Chronicles 20:21-22*

When King Jehoshaphat faced an overwhelming army, he sent out worshippers ahead of the soldiers, declaring, *"Give thanks to the Lord, for his steadfast love endures forever"* (v. 21). As they worshiped, God ambushed their enemies and gave them victory.

How to Apply:

- ✓ During rehearsals, start with high praise. Before practicing a single song, take **5** minutes to declare victory over your congregation, your city, and your church.
- ✓ Teach your team to praise before they see results. Ask: *What would your worship sound like if you already saw the breakthrough?*
- ✓ Pray and prophesy over your congregation. Expect healings, salvations, and spiritual renewal every time you lead worship.

---

2. Engaging the Congregation: Leading Beyond Performance

Worship is not a concert—it is a corporate experience where everyone should participate. Many worship leaders struggle with a disengaged congregation, but the key is leading with authority and invitation.

Exercise: The Call-and-Response Activation

Biblical Example: *Psalm 136:1-26*

This entire psalm is structured in a call-and-response style. The leader proclaims, *"Give thanks to the Lord, for He is good,"* and the people respond, *"His steadfast love endures forever."*

How to Apply:

- ✓ Incorporate moments where the congregation repeats a phrase—such as *"Hallelujah!"* or *"The Lord is good!"*
- ✓ Use intentional pauses to let the congregation respond spontaneously in their own words.

- ✓ Give them simple instructions, like *"Lift your hands," "Sing this out,"* or *"Declare this over your life."*

This helps people engage instead of observe.

---

3. Flowing with the Holy Spirit: Spontaneous Worship

The most powerful moments in worship often happen outside of the setlist. Spontaneous worship allows the Holy Spirit to lead and release prophetic breakthroughs.

Exercise: The Open Heaven Moment

Biblical Example: *Acts 16:25-26*

Paul and Silas worshiped in prison—not as a planned song, but as a response to God's greatness. As they did, the prison doors miraculously opened, showing that spontaneous worship can shift the atmosphere.

How to Apply:

- ✓ Leave room for spontaneous songs. Instead of rushing to the next song, pause and let the Spirit lead.
- ✓ Encourage your band to play softly while the congregation lifts their own song.
- ✓ Ask the Holy Spirit, "What do You want to say through worship right now?"

Many worship leaders fear the unknown, but Judah-style worship embraces the Spirit's leading.

---

4. Physical Expression: Worship with the Body

Biblical worship is not passive. The Bible is filled with **actions** of worship—lifting hands, bowing, dancing, clapping, and shouting.

Exercise: The Davidic Worship Challenge

Biblical Example: *2 Samuel 6:14*

When the Ark of the Covenant was brought to Jerusalem, King David danced before the Lord with all his might—completely unashamed. His wife, Michal, despised him for it, but David responded, *"I will celebrate before the Lord!"* (v. 21).

How to Apply:

- ✓ During team practice, challenge your team to break out of their comfort zones. If you want your congregation to express worship fully, it must start with the worship team.
- ✓ Try different expressions of worship—clapping, lifting hands, kneeling, or even dancing.
- ✓ Teach your church that worship is not just in the heart—it must be seen and heard.
- ✓ When people physically engage, their hearts follow.

---

5. Declaring Victory: Prophetic Worship

Judah-style worship is **prophetic**—it does not just react to what is happening but declares what God is about to do.

Exercise: The Prophetic Song Decree

Biblical Example: *Ezekiel 37:1-10*

God told Ezekiel to prophesy over dry bones and command them to live. As he spoke, they came to life. Worship leaders carry the same authority **to** prophesy life over a congregation**.**

How to Apply:

- ✓ Before leading worship, ask God, *"What do You want to release today?"*
- ✓ Speak out prophetic declarations before a song:
- *"Today, God is breaking chains!"*
- *"This is a place of healing!"*

- *"No weapon formed against us will prosper!"*
- ✓ Sing spontaneous songs of victory. Even if it's a simple melody, a prophetic song can unlock miracles.

---

6. Breaking Religious Routine: The Fresh Fire Challenge

Routine kills passion. If worship becomes predictable, it loses power. Judah-style worship is fresh, passionate, and unpredictable.

Exercise: The Unscripted Setlist

Biblical Example: *Mark 7:6-7*

Jesus rebuked the Pharisees for worshiping with their lips but not their hearts. True worship must be authentic and alive.

How to Apply:

- ✓ Once a month, lead a worship night with NO setlist. Let the team rely on the Holy Spirit.
- ✓ Introduce new songs and new expressions regularly. Keep worship fresh.
- ✓ Encourage testimonies between songs. When people hear real-life stories of God's goodness, it stirs faith.

Final Words: Worship That Leads to Breakthrough

Worship leaders are spiritual warriors. Judah-style worship is not just about songs—it is about leading people into encounters with God. When worship is done in faith, with passion, and with prophetic authority, chains break, lives change, and heaven touches earth.

As a worship leader, your role is to be more than a singer—you are a leader of breakthrough, bringing people into the manifest presence of God.

Reflection Questions

- ✓ *What changes can you make in your worship leading to engage the congregation more effectively?*
- ✓ *How can you prepare your heart to lead worship with greater faith and expectation?*
- ✓ *What physical expressions of worship do you need to embrace more boldly?*
- ✓ *Have you left room for spontaneous worship and the Holy Spirit's leading?*
- ✓ *What prophetic declarations can you begin incorporating into your worship leading?*

Send Judah First!
A Song of Praise

Feel free to lift your voice and sing, Let your own melody rise to the King!
Praise Him loud, let Judah lead, And as you worship, His power is freed!

Stanza 1:
We lift our voices, loud and high,
To You, O Lord, enthroned on high.
Your glory shines, so bright and true,
Forever, Lord, our praise is due!

Stanza 2:
The battle's won, Your name we call,
Before You, Lord, the giants fall.
Our hands we raise, our hearts we sing,
To Judah's Lion, Mighty King!

Chorus:
Send Judah first, let praises rise,
Your power reigns above the skies!
With lifted hands, we stand in awe,
You are our strength, our King, our ROAR!

Conclusion: Sending Judah First in Your Life

From the very beginning of this journey, we have uncovered a divine strategy woven throughout Scripture—one that reveals the power of praise and its rightful place at the forefront of every battle, every struggle, and every breakthrough. It is the principle of sending Judah first. Judah, meaning "praise," was not just a tribe in Israel; it was God's divine strategy for victory. Over and over again, the Lord commanded His people to put praise ahead of their battles, to let worship lead the way before swords were drawn, and to trust that the presence of God would go before them when they lifted their voices in faith.

Why Praise Must Always Go First

Throughout this book, we have explored the undeniable truth that praise is not just a beautiful expression of love and adoration toward God, but a mighty weapon of warfare, a gateway to divine presence, and a catalyst for miracles. We have seen how King Jehoshaphat sent worshippers ahead of his army and how their praises caused confusion in the enemy's camp (2 Chronicles 20:21-22). We have witnessed how the walls of Jericho crumbled when God's people lifted a mighty shout of praise (Joshua 6:20). We have read how Paul and Silas, bound in chains in a prison cell, experienced a supernatural earthquake that set them free when they chose to worship in the midnight hour (Acts 16:25-26). In every instance, the pattern is clear—praise must always go first.

But why? Why does God insist that we begin with praise? The answer is simple: praise shifts our perspective. When we magnify God, our problems become smaller in comparison. When we declare His goodness, our hearts are strengthened in faith. When we exalt Him in the midst of trials, we invite His presence into our circumstances. Psalm 22:3 tells us that God inhabits the praises of His people. Where praise is lifted, His throne is established. And where His throne is established, victory is inevitable.

How to Implement Judah's Principle in Daily Struggles

It is easy to praise when life is going well. But what about when challenges arise? How do we send Judah first when everything in us wants to complain, fear, or retreat? The key is to make praise our first response, not our last resort.

Consider Daniel, who, even in the face of persecution and the threat of death, maintained a lifestyle of worship. When a law was issued forbidding prayer to anyone except the king, Daniel did not panic. Instead, he went to his room, opened his windows, and prayed just as he had always done, giving thanks to God (Daniel 6:10). His immediate response was praise, and because of his unwavering faith, God shut the mouths of the lions and delivered him from harm.

For us, sending Judah first means choosing to lift our voices in worship before reacting in worry. It means declaring God's faithfulness before we see the answer. It means singing songs of victory even while the battle is still raging. When the diagnosis comes, let praise be our first response. When financial struggles hit, let worship rise before worry takes root.

When relationships are strained, let songs of trust in God be lifted before we speak words of frustration. Praise must go first, not as a mere ritual, but as a declaration of trust in God's sovereignty.

A Call to Worship Leaders, Pastors, and Believers – Let Praise Lead!

To those who lead worship in churches, the call is clear: cultivate a Judah-first culture in your congregations. Teach people to praise before they plead, to worship before they weep, and to exalt before they explain their troubles. Worship is not just a segment of a church service; it is the very foundation upon which breakthroughs are built. Lead with authenticity, teach with conviction, and create an atmosphere where people encounter the presence of God through uninhibited praise.

To pastors and ministry leaders, model a life of praise. Let your response to every challenge be one of worship. Encourage your churches to become places where praise is not just an activity, but a lifestyle. Let every prayer meeting begin with thanksgiving. Let every sermon be wrapped in exaltation. Let every believer know that praise is not optional—it is essential.

To every believer reading this, the time is now. You have been equipped with the understanding of Judah's principle. It is time to put it into practice. Let praise rise in your home. Let worship be heard in your car. Let gratitude fill your workplace. Let your children see you worshiping. Let your community witness a life that declares the goodness of God, even in the storm. Let praise lead!

A Closing Prayer and Declaration Over Your Worship Journey

Heavenly Father,

We thank You for the revelation that praise is not just an act of worship, but a powerful strategy for victory. We commit today to sending Judah first in every area of our lives. When challenges arise, we will worship. When uncertainty looms, we will lift our voices in praise. When we feel weak, we will declare Your strength.

Lord, let our lives be marked by continual worship. Let our homes be filled with the sound of thanksgiving. Let our churches be places where Your presence dwells richly. Let our battles be won, not by our own strength, but by the power of praise. Teach us to walk in this principle daily, that we may live lives of victory and bring glory to Your name.

We declare today: Praise will be our first response. Worship will be our weapon. Thanksgiving will be our testimony. And the name of Jesus will always be exalted in our lives.

In Jesus' mighty name, Amen.

Reflection Questions:

- ✓ *Think of a recent challenge you faced. How did you respond? Did praise go first, or was it an afterthought? How can you shift your response in the future?*
- ✓ *What are some practical ways you can incorporate praise into your daily routine?*
- ✓ *Have you ever experienced a breakthrough that came as a result of worship? If so, how did it strengthen your faith?*

- ✓ *How can you encourage others—family, friends, or your church—to develop a lifestyle of Judah-style praise?*
- ✓ *In what areas of your life do you struggle to praise first? How can you intentionally change that starting today?*

As you go forth, may your life be a testimony of the power of sending Judah first. Let praise lead, and watch as God moves in ways beyond what you could ever imagine. Amen and Amen!

About the Author 'GERARD ASSEY'

Gerard Assey is a Graduate in Economics, a PGD in Management (HRD) and holds a Doctorate in Leadership. Gerard holds several International Qualifications in Sales, Debt Collection, Training & Teaching, and is a 'Fellow' of the prestigious 'Institute of Sales & Marketing Management'-UK, a Certified NLP Practitioner, a 'Certified Trainer', an 'Accredited Management Teacher-Behavioral Sciences', a 'Certified Competency Facilitator', a 'Certified Management Consultant'- (the International credentials of a professional management consultant, awarded in accordance with global standards of the ICMCI); and a Certification from the University of Michigan in 'Successful Negotiation: Essential Strategies and Skills'

He is also a Member of the 'National Association of Sales Professionals' backed with several years experience in varied industries, both in India and Overseas. He also holds an 'Etiquette Consultant' Certification from the USA (by Sue Fox, Author of Best Seller: 'Business Etiquette for Dummies'. She has trained some of the top celebrities' world over). He was also a recipient of a scholarship for extensive training in Japan on 'Corporate Management for India'.

Gerard Assey is 'Founder & Chief Corporate Trainer' of the Group: '**Citius, Altius, Fortius Unlimited'**- an organization that **celebrated 20 years of Glorious Service** in 2021, focusing on 3 Core Competencies:

People. Performance. Profit; in functional areas of Sales & Marketing, HR & Organizational Development, covering Recruitment, Training & Consultancy!

Having managed organizations with large Sales Forces in India & Overseas, his specialization cover extensive areas of Sales Training (All levels - Presentation, Negotiation, Key/ Strategic Accounts Management & Managerial Skills for all sectors), Bid Proposal/ Capture Planning/ Management Trainings, Retail Sales, Customer Service & Customer Retention Programs, Training for Prevention & Collection of Debt, Self & Personal Development Programs (Time Management, Teamwork & Team Building, Business Etiquette & Personal Grooming, Leadership & Managerial Skills, People Management Skills, Train-the-Trainer etc), including preparation of Custom-designed Business Manuals for Internal (HR, Induction, and Sales etc) & External use (Instruction, User Manuals).

Gerard has successfully conducted over 6430 Trainings & Workshops (as of Feb '24) all across India, Middle East, Africa, Europe & S.E. Asia. Besides public programs conducted regularly, both in India & Overseas, he has some of the top names as clients whom he services from Single Owners to large Public & Government undertakings, covering all sectors, for their in-house needs.

His website: www.CollectionSkills.com is the only one in this part of the world to be featured in the 'Collections & Credit Risk Magazine-USA' under 'Who's Who in Training' and ranks TOP, along with other websites listed below on most search engines.

Gerard is author of 174 books already (Feb 2024), all the books being available on all online platforms and outlets as E-books and Paperbacks

A few of our business related books:

1. Bite-sized Bits on Commonsense Management
2. Heart to Heart on Life's Principles'
3. How to become a Successful Manager
4. The Sales Professionals' Master Workbook of S.Y.S.T.E.M.S
5. The Professional Business Email Etiquette Handbook & Guide
6. The Professional Business Video-Conferencing Etiquette Handbook & Guide
7. Professional Presentation Skills
8. Exceptional Customer Service
9. Professional Tele-Marketing Skills
10. Professional Debt Collection Skills
11. The G.R.E.A.T. Sales & Service Workbook
12. Sales Training Advantage for Results (*The Ultimate Sales Training Manual to enable you stand out as a S.T.A.R.*)
13. CEO Daily Planner & Organizer
14. The Sales Professionals' Master Daily Planner
15. The Professional Debt Collector's Master Daily Planner
16. My Daily Planner & Organizer
17. MY EMERGENCY INFORMATION RECORD (Family Emergency & Peace of Mind Planner)
18. The Ultimate Therapist & Counselors Planner and Organizer
19. Building an Ethical Workplace
20. Managing Relationships at Work
21. Managing Business Meetings Effectively
22. Effective Delegation Skills
23. Goal Setting for Success
24. B2B Selling by Email
25. Professional Business Etiquette & Grooming
26. Dining Etiquette & Table Manners
27. Effective Networking Skills
28. Grooming, Etiquette & Manners for Teens, Young Adults & Future Leaders
29. Inter-Personal Skills
30. Get Ready, Get Hired!
31. Selling in a Recession

32. Effective Receivables Management in an Economic Downturn!
33. Real Estate & Property Sales Training
34. Credit Sales & Accounts Receivable Management
35. Selling Skills for Real Estate & Property Advisors
36. Take G.R.E.A.T. C.A.R.E!
37. Spa, Salon & Health Club Selling Skills
38. Selling Travel, Holiday & MICE Services
39. Selling Skills for Spa's, Salons & Health Clubs
40. Retailing in Salons & Spas
41. Selling Holiday, Vacation, Tours & Packages
42. The Power of Sales Referrals
43. Selling Luxury
44. Technical Selling Skills
45. Financial Advisors Sales Training
46. Dealing with Burnout at Work Monopolize Your Markets
47. Selling to Affluent Customers
48. Growing up with Grace
49. Financial Selling Skills
50. *The Effective Manager's Guide: Key Skills to Thrive*
51. From Aspiring to Inspiring: A Guide for New Managers on the Rise
52. The Power of Focus
53. Selling with Integrity: Sell Like Jesus The Perfect Role Model!
54. 31 Habits of Champions: Your 31-Day Journey to Greatness
55. Rejecting Grasshopper Talk: From Grasshopper to Giant-Killer-*Defeating Giants Daily!*
56. Navigate the AI-Powered Future of Bid & Proposals: Up-Skill to Stay Relevant with Alternative Career Paths & Opportunities
57. Hiring Sales Winners
58. Present with Impact
59. Success Unlocked: *Breaking Free from Habits that Hold You Back*
60. Complaints to Cheers, Feedback to Gold: Mastering Complaints Management
61. Thriving Together: *Cultivating Diversity, Equity, and Inclusion*
62. Coaching Skills for Sales Managers

63. Soaring to Success in Business & Leadership: Swifter, Higher, Stronger!
64. From Classroom to Podium: A Student's Guide to Powerful Public Speaking & Presentation Skills
65. Developing Self-Discipline
66. The CEO's 31-Day Power Plan: Unlocking Success through Essential Traits
67. Credibility Matters
68. A Winning Attitude
69. Bid & Proposal Management Using AI
70. Sales Forecasting: A Practical & Proven Guide to Strategic Sales Forecasting
71. Elevate & Energize: *50 Dynamic & Fun Activities for Peak Workplace Morale*
72. 'Sales SOS! Sales on Fire! *30 Days to Conquer Chaos & the Nightmares of Success!'*
73. Mastering Sales Managerial Skills: *Building High-Performing Teams & Driving Exceptional Results*
74. Eagle-Eyed Leadership: Unleashing the Power of 31 Lessons from Eagles
75. The Ultimate Employee Training Guide: *Training Today, Leading Tomorrow*
76. Being More Accountable at Work
77. Creating a Culture of Continuous Improvement
78. Effective Questioning & Listening Skills
79. The Power of Value Selling
80. The Growth Mindset
81. Mastering Professional Help Desk Skills
82. The Power to Lead with Empathy
83. Being Prepared: The Key to Unlocking Success
84. Youthful Spark-Youth Energizers, Activities and Games-Igniting the Fun in Youth
85. Ignite your Motivation for Success
86. Elevate Your Executive Presence: *Your Roadmap to Executive Excellence*
87. Smart Decisions: *Mastering Problem Solving with Strategic Solutions for Business Success*
88. Strategic Planning: *Developing and Implementing Strategic Plans to Achieve Long-Term Business Goals*
89. The Power of Stay Interviews
90. Developing G.R.I.T.
91. Adaptability

92. Diagnosis- *A Key Skill for Leadership*
93. The Burnout-Proof Salesperson: *The Master Guide to Preventing Stress & Burnout*- Strategies for Thriving in Sales
94. Learning from Failure: *Keys to Success*
95. Customer Success Management
96. Overcoming the Killers of Motivation
97. The C-Suite Code: *Mastering Skills for Executive Excellence'*
98. Dealing with Difficult Customers
99. Unlocking Your Potential: Mastering the Top 20 Life Skills for a Brighter Future

100. Nurturing Tomorrow's Leaders: *Essential Soft Skills Every Child Must Learn*

101. Lively & Fun Party Games for Seniors & Elders

102. Role Playing for Sales Champions: From Practice to Performance

103. Fun and Exciting Party Games for Kids

104. Case Studies for Sales

105. Role-Playing for Unbeatable Customer Service

106. Case Studies in Customer Service

107. Case Studies in Winning Negotiations

108. Case Studies in Management & Leadership

109. Case Studies in Human Resources & Talent Management

110. CEO Success Blueprint: The Essential Toolkit for CEOs and C-Level Executives

111. The Salesperson's Self-Coaching Guide: *Master Your Own Self-Coaching Plan for Success*

112. Overcoming Procrastination: *Your Ultimate Guide to Stop Delaying and Start Living Your Best Life*

113. When True Colors Are Exposed: *The Journey to Unmasking Humanity*

114. Life-Changing Habits for Teens: Teen Success Blueprint for a Bright Future

115. Workplace Stress-Free: *Proven Strategies to Thrive at Work and Beyond*

From the Ministry side, Gerard graduated in the very first batch of Charis Bible College-India & had for over 9 years served as a Part-time Faculty at Charis Bible College-Chennai (Andrew Wommack Ministries-Colorado, USA).

He is also a graduate of the Advanced Mentorship Program (AMP) and the Circle Of Ministerial Engagement (C.O.M.E.) of Prophet Jerome Fernando and a Spiritual Son of the Esteemed Prophet.

An accomplished author of several Secular & Christian Books, Gerard has been on the board of a few international organizations and boasts of being the SON of the MOST HIGH GOD: An ordinary guy following an extraordinary GOD!

...And some of his most recent Christian Books being:

1. A Bouquet of Praises for My KING
2. Christian Jokes for the Serious Religious' Folks!
3. Jesus Healed You!
4. Praise24Ever! (also in Tamil version)
5. The 5G Network of GOD
6. Building Faith over F.E.A.R- FACE EVERYTHING AND RISE with JESUS
7. Hebrew and Greek Praise and Worship Words
8. Godly Mothers' and Grandmothers' Bible Story time for Kids!
9. Miracles of Jesus in Pictures
10. Raise your Praise all 365 Days
11. Thanking GOD with an Attitude of Gratitude
12. Meditating on the Attributes of GOD
13. Puppet Scripts
14. Alcohol Ruins, JESUS Reforms, Renews & Restores!
15. Habakkuk 2:2 Christian Daily Journal, Planner & Organizer
16. ABC of GOD's Word for Handwriting Practice
17. Daily Bible Verse Handwriting Practice (Building Godly Character & Faith through Cursive Handwriting Practice!)
18. Guiding Light: Fun & Faith-Building Bible Activities for Children
19. Rejecting Grasshopper Talk: From Grasshopper to Giant-Killer-*Defeating Giants Daily!*
20. Teen Titans of Faith: *Building Courage, Determination & Christ-like-Esteem*
21. I AM Empowered: *Unleashing Divine Power with Positive Declarations*
22. Be A Solution Provider-*From Passion to Purpose: A Biblical*

Guide to Being the Answer to the World!

23. Miracles of JESUS
24. Parables of Jesus for a Meaningful Life!
25. A Grateful Heart: Importance of Sharing Testimonies of GOD's Grace
26. Melodies of Worship to JESUS: 31 Songs of Praise & Worship From My Heart to HIS!
27. I AM SO BLESSED!
28. My Daily Cup of Energizer
29. 31 Leadership Lessons *from* Jesus- *The Supreme Leader*
30. Peace Amidst Storms: A Biblical Guide to Conquering S.T.R.E.S.S.
31. Rise Above: 20 Biblical Eagle Lessons for Life's Triumphs
32. Godly Goal Setting: *The FAITHFUL Blueprint for a Purpose-Driven Life*
33. The Profound Attributes of our Mighty GOD: Understanding the 10S's of the Almighty
34. Worship Now, Worship Forever: *A Journey from Earthly Praise to Eternal Glory*
35. Unceasing Praise & Worship: *365 Days to Worship the King*
36. Awakening Praise & Worship: Hebrew & Greek Words to Raise Your Praise
37. Sing a NEW Song to the LORD Everyday: *Daily Devotions of Praise & Worship to Lift Your Heart & Glorify HIS Name*
38. *The* A.R.O.M.A. of True Worship: *Creating Worship That Delights God*
39. Becoming A Kingdom Champion: *Embracing God's Call for a Life of Purpose & Victory*
40. The Busy Businessman's Daily Devotional: 366 Crisp Truths to Start Your Day Strong
41. The Teacher's Heart: *Daily Devotions for Educators*
42. Anchored! *A 31-Day Devotional for Students Facing Life's Challenges*
43. Suddenly! Unlocking Unorthodox Breakthroughs through Unusual Worship
44. Overcoming Adversity: *Lessons from the Bible for Modern Challenges*
45. LORD, Don't do it without me
46. Kingdom Leadership: *Biblical Principles for Modern Leaders*
47. Heartprints of God- *Growing God's Way:* Daily Devotions for Kids to Shine Bright
48. Send Judah First: Let your Praises Go up First to See the Mighty Move of GOD

Besides regularly contributing to business & trade journals, including international ones such as the 'Creative Training Techniques' and the 'Sales News' of the U.S.A, He is also a member of several prestigious bodies & trade associations, having participated in many Conferences & Workshops in India & Overseas.

Prior to his last assignment of leading & managing a large MNC as head, Gerard had a 3-year stint in the Middle East as a Consultant with a leading British Consultancy Firm.

As the past 'Official Country Representative' for the International Business Award- 'THE STEVIES'-(the business world's own Oscar) for about 4 years- he ensured a few Indian companies that qualify for the same every year!

Gerard can be contacted at:
Email: training@Sales-Training.in,training@CollectionSkills.com
Websites:

www.Sales-Training.in
www.EtiquetteWorks.in
www.CollectionSkills.com
www.RetailSalesTraining.in
www.SalesTrainingIndia.com
www.ManualPreparation.com
www.TrainingWithPuppets.com
www.FirstContactAcademy.com
www.SalesAndMarketingRecruiter.com

Our TRAININGS that can help your team

- ✓ **Sales Effectiveness**: Selling Skills for any Sector: Service/ Logistics/ FMCG Realty/ Insurance & Finance/ Media/ SPA's, Health Clubs & Salons/ Key Account Management, Effective Negotiation Skills/ Bid & Proposal Management Skills/ Retail Sales Training: Any Sector (Auto, Jewelry, Clothing, Luxury etc)
- ✓ **Customer Service Skills**-Complaints Handling & Customer Retention
- ✓ **Debt Prevention & Collection Skills**
- ✓ **Etiquette & Grooming**
- ✓ **Leadership & Managerial Skills**
- ✓ **Self & Personal Development Skills**: Presentation Skills/ Effective Communication Skills/Business Proposal Writing Skills/ Problem Solving & Decision Making Skills/ Empowering Secretaries-The perfect PA! (For Secretaries & PA's)/ Effective Time Management/ Teamwork & Teambuilding/ P.R.I.D.E- **P**ersonal **R**esponsibility **I**n **D**elivering **E**xcellence

www.ingramcontent.com/pod-product-compliance
Ingram Content Group UK Ltd.
Pitfield, Milton Keynes, MK11 3LW, UK
UKHW021341190726
13845UKWH00027B/658

9 788198 351531